SKUNKS

NORTH AMERICAN ANIMAL DISCOVERY LIBRARY

Lynn M. Stone

Rourke Corporation, Inc.
Vero Beach, Florida 32964

PHOTO CREDITS

© Lynn M. Stone: Pages 1, 4, 7, 10, 15, 17, 18, 21
© Tom and Pat Leeson: Pages 8, 12, 13
© Karen Dawn Ward: Page 21

ACKNOWLEDGEMENTS

The author thanks the following for photographic assistance
with a portion of this book: Brookfield Zoo, Brookfield, Illinois

LIBRARY OF CONGRESS
Library of Congress Cataloging-in-Publication Data
Stone, Lynn M.
  Skunks / by Lynn M. Stone.

  p. cm. — (North American animal discovery library)
  Summary: Discusses the physical characteristics, habitat,
and behavior of the skunk.
  ISBN 0-86593-046-5
  1. Skunks—Juvenile literature. [1. Skunks.] I. Title. II. Series:
Stone, Lynn M. North American animal discovery library.
QL737.C25S76   1990
599.74'447—dc20   89-77834
                                        CIP
                                        AC

Skunk

TABLE OF CONTENTS

THE SKUNK

Skunks are small animals, but they carry a big weapon.

A skunk's weapon is a smelly spray called **musk.** A skunk uses musk to defend itself.

Musk smells awful! People and other big animals treat skunks with respect.

A skunk has about one tablespoon of the oily, yellow musk. It squirts the musk from grape-sized **glands** under its tail. A skunk can hit another animal 15 feet away.

The striped skunk *(Mephitis mephitis)* is the most common American skunk.

Striped skunk in Florida

THE SKUNK'S COUSINS

The striped skunk's closest cousins are three other kinds, or **species,** of skunks. They are the hooded skunk *(Mephitis macroura),* spotted skunk *(Spilogale putorius),* and hog-nosed skunk *(Conepatus mesoleucus).*

Skunks are related to weasels, badgers, minks, ferrets, otters, fishers, wolverines, and martens. Like skunks, these are meat-eating mammals with shiny fur, short legs, small, rounded ears, and musk glands.

Their musk is not as strong-smelling to people as the skunk's, however.

River otter

HOW THEY LOOK

Skunks have bushy tails and long fur. They look larger than they really are.

The spotted skunk is the smallest of the skunks. It can be little more than a foot long. The big hog-nosed skunk can reach three feet in length.

Skunks have pointed noses with flat tops. They have sharp claws for digging.

Skunks are black and white. Each kind of skunk has fur in a special pattern of spots or stripes.

Striped skunk in Washington

WHERE THEY LIVE

Skunks of one kind or another live throughout the United States and southern Canada.

The striped skunk lives in almost all of the United States and the southern half of Canada.

The striped skunk lives in deserts, forests, and grasslands. It also lives near some towns.

The little spotted skunk lives in much of the United States, too. The hooded skunk and the hog-nosed skunk live in the Southwest.

Striped skunks
like open woodland

Fisher

Badger

HOW THEY LIVE

They move rather slowly as they prowl about. Skunks never seem to be in a hurry. Perhaps they feel safe with their own brand of "perfume."

Like their many cousins, skunks stay awake and active almost all year. They rarely fall into deep winter sleep.

Spotted skunks are quicker than the larger skunks. They are also good climbers.

*Striped skunk
in hollow log*

THE SKUNK'S BABIES

Baby skunks are born in a group, or litter, of from two to ten in the spring. They are blind at birth, but they have some fur.

They live in a hole in the ground or in a hollow place, often between rocks.

By summer, the young skunks look like their parents. They go off on their own in the fall.

Skunks in captivity usually live to be six. One skunk, however, lived to be twelve.

Striped skunk

PREDATOR AND PREY

Skunks are **omnivores** because they eat both plants and animals.

The hog-nosed skunk uses its nose to root for insects. Like other skunks, it also eats small mammals, some vegetables and fruit, and small reptiles.

When skunks hunt other animals they are **predators.** The animals they catch are **prey.**

Most animals avoid skunks. The powerful great horned owl often makes the skunk its prey. The owl must not have a good sense of smell.

Great horned owl

THE SKUNK AND PEOPLE

Almost everyone has smelled a skunk. The odor can carry for more than one mile.

Skunks spray musk if they are frightened. People should give skunks plenty of room so that they don't feel afraid.

There is another reason to stay clear of skunks. Now and then skunks carry rabies, a very serious disease.

Skunks are not trapped often, but the fur of the spotted skunk is sometimes used in clothing.

Spotted skunk in defensive position for spraying

THE SKUNK'S FUTURE

Many wild animals have become **endangered.** They are in danger of disappearing forever. Skunks are not endangered.

Skunks live in many different kinds of dens. They even live under old buildings. And they eat many different foods. If the clearing of land removes a favorite food, they can eat another.

Striped skunks may even live in your neighborhood. They like to root for insects on lawns.

If you find a skunk hunting, watch and enjoy it—but keep your distance!

Glossary

endangered (en DANE jerd)—in danger of no longer existing; very rare

gland (GLAND)—a body pouch which stores some type of liquid

musk (MUHSK)—A strong-smelling liquid made by certain animals

nocturnal (nohk TUR nal)—active at night

omnivore (OHM nih vore)—an animal which eats both plants and animals

predator (PRED a tor)—an animal that kills other animals for food

prey (PRAY)—an animal that is hunted by another for food

species (SPEE sheez)—within a group of closely related animals, one certain kind

INDEX